This is a work of fiction. Names, characters, places, and incidents are products of the author's imagination. Any resemblance to actual persons, living or dead, business establishments, events, or locales is entirely coincidental.

Book design and cover by Calvin Reynolds
Jayce A Bee Adventure text and illustrations Copyright ©2015 Calvin Reynolds All rights reserved.

Published in 2017 by Concepts Redefined, an imprint of Calvin Reynolds
All rights reserved.

Jayce A Bee Adventure

Copyright ©2015 Calvin Reynolds All rights reserved.
No part of this book may be reproduced, stored in a retrieval system, or transmitted by any means without the written permission of the author

PART ONE

QUEST FOR MR. CRIX

It was the middle of summer, and the Beetopia colony was buzzing with excitement.
Nectar and pollen filled the air, as joyful honeybees buzzed throughout the Enchanted Forest.

Two friends named Jayce and Dex were on their pollen route.
Jayce didn't have a stinger like all the other bees.
He was often teased, but that never stopped him
from being courageous and adventurous.

Dex admired Jayce for standing up for himself when other bees would bully and tease him for not having a stinger. Dex was a quick thinker and always there to help Jayce out of sticky situations.

After a long day, Dex glanced over his shoulder and said,
"Jayce, we better head home before it gets dark."
Jayce smiled and responded,
"Time flies when you're having fun! Let's get going!"

When Jayce and Dex returned to Beetopia, the wasp king and his minions had stolen the most crucial element of the bees' survival, the Nectcia Jewel! Dex began to panic as Jayce gazed speechless in disbelief.

The Nectcia Jewel is the source of Beetopia's prosperity. It has the ability to generate large amounts of honey from nectar. King Zeek and his minions would stop at nothing to gain possession of the magical device.

Queen Zoey, leader of Beetopia, announced to the crowd.
"We need volunteers to reclaim Beetopia's most valuable jewel."
There was silence.
No one was willing to attempt such a difficult task.

The mission at hand seemed impossible, but Jayce knew he had the one thing all the other bees lacked—courage.

"I will try!" Jayce shouted.
"Who spoke?" the Queen asked.
"It was me, Jayce. My friend Dex and I will try!"
Dex was shocked that Jayce dragged him into volunteering.
"Come forth!" Queen Zoey demanded.

As Jayce approached the Queen, a voice yelled out,
"Look, he doesn't have a stinger!"
"We're doomed!" another voice shouted.
Jayce didn't allow the teasing to discourage him.

Queen Zoey held up her arm signaling all talking to stop.
She smiled at the two brave honeybees.
"The fate of Beetopia now rest in your hands," she said.

The next morning, Queen Zoey approached Jayce and said,
"Find the old cricket named Mr. Crix.
He can help you."
With that advice, Jayce and Dex flew off into the forest.

**The two friends were on their way until Jayce suddenly heard a voice crying for help.
It was a ladybug trapped in a spider's web.
"Please help me!" she exclaimed.**

The spider was eager to snack on his captured meal.
"We can't leave her!" Jayce declared.
He courageously began distracting the spider by yelling and throwing pebbles, while Dex nervously pried her loose.
Once she was free, they quickly escaped.

"Thank you both for saving me. I'm Lilly!"
the ladybug announced.
Jayce explained that they were looking for Mr. Crix.
To show gratitude, Lilly offered to
help find his whereabouts.

Meanwhile, the Wasps' Lair was buzzing with excitement. Delicious honey would soon be overflowing throughout the nest. Beetopia's prized possession now belonged to them.

King Zeek was overjoyed with thoughts of tasty honey.
"Now that we have the Nectcia Jewel, I want to start making honey as soon as possible!" he demanded.

While Jayce, Dex, and Lilly wandered through the forest, a menacing group of dragonflies spotted them. "Come back here!" the dragonflies shouted, as they began to chase the three friends.

As they flew away, Lilly fell behind.
"Wait, don't leave me!" Lilly cried out.
Jayce bravely turned around and allowed
Lilly to quickly climb onto his back.

The dragonflies chased them until there was nowhere to run.
Jayce and his friends braced themselves
as the dragonflies closed in.
Suddenly, a mysterious figure appeared
and frightened them away.

"What are you three doing in these parts of the forest?" the kind stranger asked.
"We're looking for Mr. Crix. We need his help!" Jayce explained.
"I know where he is!" the stranger replied with a smile.

Lilly asked, "Why are you smiling?"
"Well, young lady, I'm Mr. Crix." he announced.
Jayce, Dex, and Lilly were shocked.
The first part of their quest was accomplished,
but the hardest part was yet to come.

PART TWO

HEROES OF BEETOPIA

Mr. Crix explained the numbing effects of the mysterious tree sap called Treesha. "This substance is your best defense against those menacing wasps," Mr. Crix said.

The wise cricket also created special gadgets that would help them retrieve the Nectcia Jewel from the Wasps' Lair.

For Lilly, he crafted a small boomerang called Wind Dasher. It was perfect for her small hands.

He made Dex a slingshot called Oak Slinger, capable of slinging small blobs of Treesha.

Because of his courage, Mr. Crix granted Jayce the Treesha Brace, a wrist device that could generate and propel Treesha.

Mr Crix warned that when the orbs turn red, the brace would need time to refill.

Without haste, the trio traveled to the Wasps' Lair.
When they arrived, Jayce and Dex
entered the domain, while Lilly stayed behind.
Once Jayce spotted the Nectcia Jewel, they hid quietly
as King Zeek and his minions napped.

Dex was nervous and afraid.
Jayce looked him right in the eyes and said,
"Beetopia is depending on us! I believe we can do this!"
Dex felt relieved and began to gather himself.

Jayce whispered to Dex,
"Keep a lookout while I grab the Nectcia Jewel."
As Jayce slowly approached the magical gem,
a large shadow began to loom behind him.

"Where do you think you're going with my jewel?"
King Zeek questioned.
Jayce looked at the gruesome king and shouted,
"This belongs to Beetopia, and I'm taking it back home!"

Jayce sprayed the mad king with Treesha.
The wasps' leader splashed into the pool of honey
below causing the other wasps to awaken.
"After them!" screamed King Zeek.

Jayce and Dex used their Treesha gadgets to neutralize swarms of angry wasps as they scrambled to escape.

Lilly spotted her two friends and positioned her Wind Dasher. "Now, Lilly! Now!" Jayce yelled.

Lilly threw her Wind Dasher with striking accuracy.
It cut through vines that held back petals full of gooey Treesha.
Tons of Treesha came pouring down on the trailing wasps.

"You'll pay for this you pesky bee!"
Before Zeek could utter another word,
a big blob of Treesha plopped right on his head.

The three companions safely escaped.
"We did it! We did it!" they cheered.
They laughed and celebrated while
returning home to Beetopia.

When they arrived, many bees were shocked and stared in disbelief.
Jayce flashed a smile of confidence at the doubtful bees that teased him for not having a stinger.

Jayce approached the Queen beaming with joy.
"Your Highness, I believe this belongs to you,"
Jayce said as he pulled the jewel from his backpack.
The crowd erupted in joyful cheer.

The queen was overjoyed as she spoke to the crowd. "Citizens of Beetopia, these three heroes are examples that bravery starts from believing in yourself."
The crowd let out a thunderous applause.

There were celebrations in honor of Jayce and his friends. King Zeek and his minions may return one day. However, Beetopia's most courageous bee will be ready when the time comes.

—The End—

BEE-LIEVE YOU CAN AND YOU WILL!
JAYCE THE BEE BOOKS
Written & Illustrated by Calvin Reynolds

Available at **amazon** · **BARNES&NOBLE.com** · **JAYCETHEBEE.COM** · **BAM! Books-A-Million**

Most Online Distribution Channels

COPYRIGHT © ALL RIGHTS RESERVED

www.ingramcontent.com/pod-product-compliance
Lightning Source LLC
LaVergne TN
LVHW071027070426
835507LV00002B/56